BATTER

By Jason Glaser

Must Read!

Gareth Stevens
Publishing

Please visit our Web site, www.garethstevens.com. For a free color catalog of all our high-quality books, call toll free 1-800-542-2595 or fax 1-877-542-2596.

Library of Congress Cataloging-in-Publication Data

Glaser, Jason.
 Batter / Jason Glaser.
    p. cm. — (Play ball. Baseball)
 Includes index.
 ISBN 978-1-4339-4620-2 (pbk.)
 ISBN 978-1-4339-4621-9 (6-pack)
 ISBN 978-1-4339-4619-6 (library binding)
 1. Batting (Baseball)—Juvenile literature. 2. Baseball players—United States—Juvenile literature.   I. Title.
 GV869.G63 2011
 796.357'26—dc22

                                    2010039132

First Edition

Published in 2011 by
Gareth Stevens Publishing
111 East 14th Street, Suite 349
New York, NY 10003

Copyright © 2011 Gareth Stevens Publishing

Designer: Dan Hosek
Editor: Greg Roza

Photo credits: Cover, pp. 1, 19, 36 Otto Greule Jr./Getty Images; (cover, back cover, pp. 2–3, 5, 7–8, 11, 12, 15, 17, 18–19, 21, 22, 25, 26, 37, 38–39, 41, 42–43, 44–45, 46–47, 48 background image on all), pp. 41, 43 Shutterstock.com; p. 4 Jerry Wachter/Sports Illustrated/Getty Images; p. 5 Focus On Sport/Getty Images; p. 6 Diamond Images/Getty Images; p. 7 (bottom image) Buyenlarge/Getty Images; pp. 7 (bat), 11, 29 Transcendental Graphics/Getty Images; p. 8 New York Times Co./Getty Images; p. 9 Walter Iooss Jr./Sports Illustrated/Getty Images; p. 10 Pictorial Parade/Getty Images; pp. 12, 13, 15 Hulton Archive/Getty Images; p. 14 Getty Images; p. 16 Ronald Martinez/Getty Images; p. 17 Andrew Burton/Getty Images; pp. 18, 26, 34 Dilip Vishwanat/Getty Images; p. 20 Christian Petersen/Getty Images; pp. 21, 31, 37 Jim McIsaac/Getty Images; pp. 22, 30 Jonathan Daniel/Getty Images; p. 23 Stephen Dunn/Getty Images; p. 24 Kevin C. Cox/Getty Images; p. 25 Nick Latham/Getty Images; p. 27 Doug Pensinger/Getty Images; p. 28 J. Meric/Getty Images; p. 32 Jamie Squire/Getty Images; p. 33 Jeff Gross/Getty Images; pp. 35, 38 Jed Jacobsohn/Getty Images; p. 39 Lisa Blumenfeld/Getty Images; p. 40 Andersen Ross/Photodisc/Getty Images; p. 42 Erik Isakson/Blend Images/Getty Images; p. 44 John G. Zimmerman/Sports Illustrated/Getty Images; p. 45 Eliot J. Schechter/Getty Images.

Printed in the United States of America

CPSIA compliance information: Batch #CW11GS: For further information contact Gareth Stevens, New York, New York at 1-800-542-2595.

CONTENTS

Boldface words appear in the glossary.

CARRY A BIG STICK

In baseball, **offense** begins at home plate. Each batter stands alone, looking for a chance to run up the score as their teammates run the bases.

The Big Moment

It's the moment every young baseball player dreams about. The World Series is on the line. There are runners on all three bases, but your team has two outs. This was the situation Kent Hrbek faced as he came up to bat in the sixth **inning** of Game Six of the 1987 World Series. His Minnesota Twins were down three games to two against the St. Louis Cardinals. Losing the game meant losing the series.

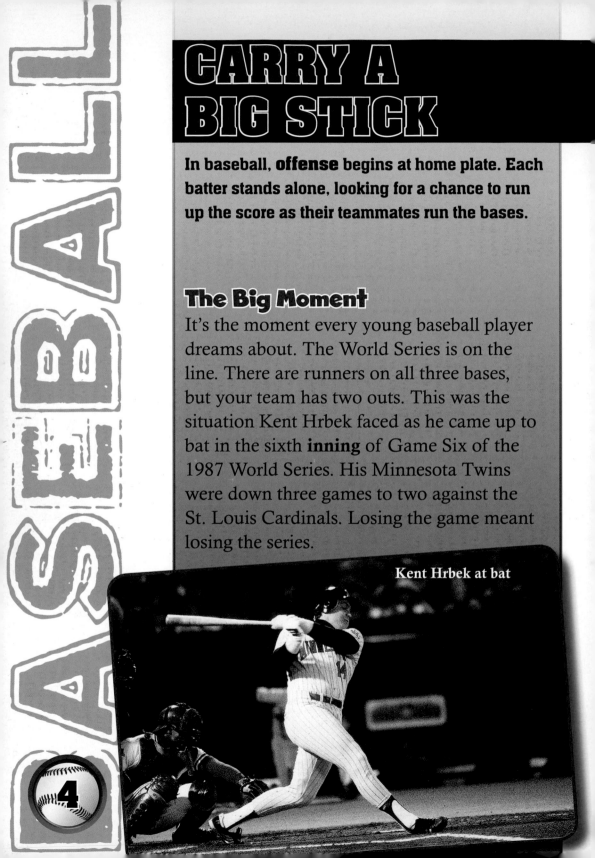

Kent Hrbek at bat

The game was close, with the Twins leading 6–5. Guessing that the pitcher would start with a fastball, Hrbek swung at the first pitch and slammed it over the outfield fence. Just like that, four runs scored, and the Twins led 10–5. The Twins won the game and continued on to win game seven for the first World Series championship in the team's history.

Batters are the only source of offense on a baseball team. Let's learn more about how batters win baseball games.

Not only did Hrbek hit a famous home run during Game Six, he also got the last out of the game at first base, too.

01

Baseball Is a Big Hit

The stick is one of the oldest toys in human history. Children have swung sticks against pretend enemies and real rocks for centuries. The ball had probably been invented just a short time before someone tried to see how far they could hit it with a stick.

The Game of Ball

In the earliest ball games of young America, the action started only after a player hit the ball. Players swung shaped wooden bats similar to those used in the British game of cricket. These "strikers" told the ball thrower, or "feeder," where and how to pitch the ball so they could hit it easily.

This picture from the 1840s shows children playing a game similar to baseball.

The first official baseball leagues began in the 1850s. Within just a few decades, winning and losing had become serious business. Pitchers no longer threw easy balls to the batters, but rather they tried to get batters out by throwing hard-to-hit balls. As the battle between pitcher and batter became more heated, the rules about pitches, balls, and bats increased.

Wooden Bats

One thing that's never changed is that all professional baseball bats are wooden. The metal bats youth and college teams use hit balls farther, but tradition has kept wooden bats in the pros.

One of the first professional baseball games, shown here, was played in Hoboken, New Jersey.

7

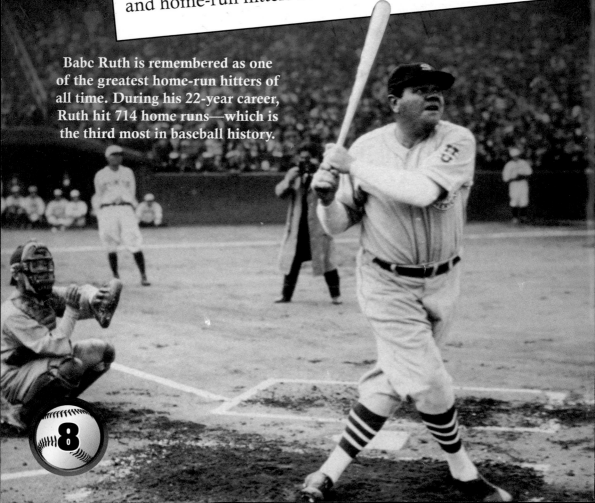

Ball games were soon played in ballparks instead of open fields. These parks had fences that fans sat behind to watch the game. Some players could hit balls over the fences and into the stands. These were home runs that allowed the batter to score by running all the way around the bases without being put out by the other team. Any other teammates already on base also crossed home plate and scored during a home run. Hitting long balls proved popular, and home-run hitters became crowd favorites.

Babe Ruth is remembered as one of the greatest home-run hitters of all time. During his 22-year career, Ruth hit 714 home runs—which is the third most in baseball history.

The Designated Hitter

Teams faced a tough decision when they had a good hitter who was aging or couldn't play in the field. In 1973, the American League made a rule allowing teams to have one player who could hit in place of a weak hitter, usually the pitcher. This player was called the designated hitter, and the rule let great hitters keep playing even if they couldn't play **defense**.

On April 6, 1973, Ron Blomberg of the New York Yankees became the first designated hitter in the history of Major League Baseball (MLB).

Home-Field Advantage

The American League uses the designated-hitter rule, but the National League doesn't. During the World Series or **interleague** games, the home team's league rules are used.

9

02

The Kings of Swing

As the rules of baseball began favoring batting over pitching, the greatest hitters in history began to appear.

The Georgia Peach

Ty Cobb maintained a career **batting average** that players since have wished they could maintain for even one season. Between 1905 and 1928, Cobb averaged a .366 batting average, mostly with the Detroit Tigers. It's the highest lifetime average of any player, and Cobb did it against some of the toughest pitchers in history.

Cobb was from Narrows, Georgia. When sportswriter Grantland Rice saw him play in Augusta, Georgia, he called Cobb the "Georgia Peach." The name stuck.

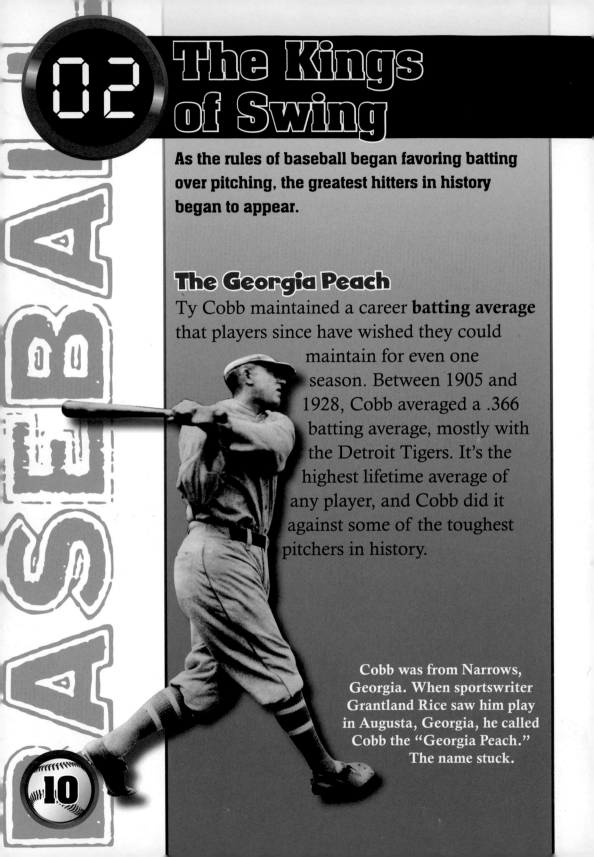

BASEBALL

Two of the greatest hitters in the history of baseball played during the same years but never faced each other. Race kept them apart. However, some fans recognized their equal levels of greatness and gave them nicknames comparing them to each other.

George Herman "Babe" Ruth is probably the most famous baseball player who ever lived. At the end of his career in 1935, he had a lifetime **slugging percentage** of .690—a record that still stands. He hit 714 home runs in his career, including 60 in one season. Yet fans who saw Ruth and African American Josh Gibson play knew that Gibson was at least as good—maybe better. So they called Ruth the "White Josh Gibson."

In the 1930s, society forced whites and African Americans to live separately. As a result, Gibson was forced to play in the **Negro League**. Although records weren't well kept, many believe Gibson hit nearly 800 home runs during his career. He became famous as the "Black Babe Ruth."

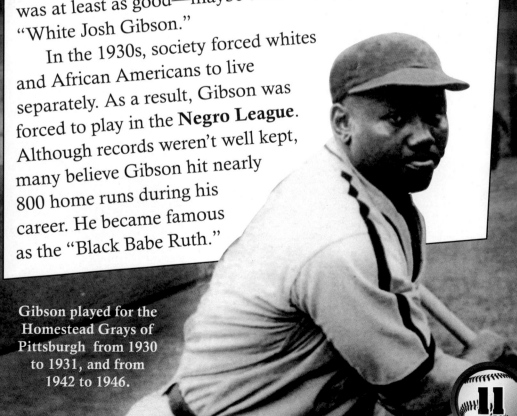

Gibson played for the Homestead Grays of Pittsburgh from 1930 to 1931, and from 1942 to 1946.

11

In the 13 years that Joe DiMaggio played with the New York Yankees, they won the World Series nine times. Their success was in large part due to DiMaggio's dependable hitting. In 1941, DiMaggio's masterful swing let him get safely on base for 56 games in a row. This extremely hard feat is one of the most highly regarded records in baseball.

DiMaggio earned the nickname "Joltin' Joe" because he hit with such power. He was also called the "Yankee Clipper" because he was quick and graceful, like the fast sailing ships called "clippers."

12

The Boston Red Sox's Ted Williams was a lifelong student of the art of hitting. Williams practiced swinging all the time, sometimes taking pretend swings while playing in the outfield. Between 1939 and 1960, he racked up 521 home runs and the best **on-base percentage** ever in baseball. His batting average of .406 in 1941 was the last time any hitter reached an average over .400 in a season.

Williams earned the nickname the "Splendid Splinter" because he was thin and was a great batter.

The Triple Crown

Batters who have the highest batting average, number of home runs, and **RBI**s in one season are said to win the "triple crown." It's only happened 16 times—Williams did it twice.

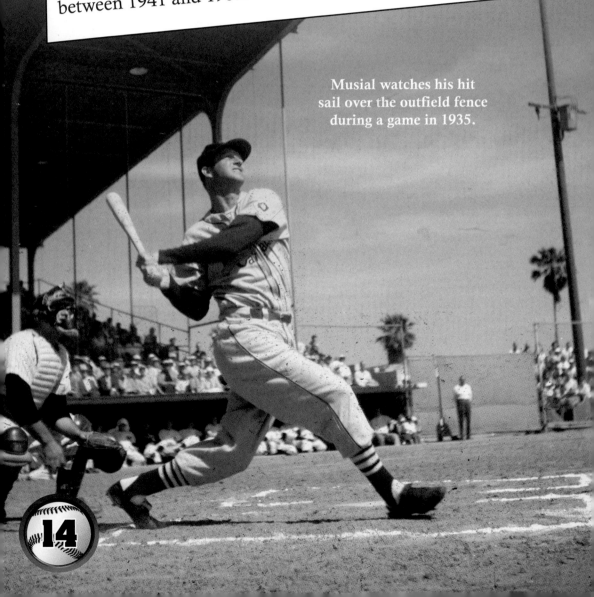

Stan the Man

For more than 2 decades, Stan Musial was the backbone of the St. Louis Cardinals. He was a quick, all-purpose hitter who not only clubbed home runs but often led the league in **doubles** and **triples**. Musial's leadership helped bring three World Series championships to St. Louis. He was also an All-Star nearly every season he played—20 times between 1941 and 1963.

Musial watches his hit sail over the outfield fence during a game in 1935.

14

No one has brought more runners safely home than Henry "Hank" Aaron. His mighty bat drove home 2,297 runs between 1954 and 1976—an all-time record. Many came from his 755 career homers.

Those home runs contributed to his 1,477 extra-base hits, which is another record.

Though some were angry when Aaron—an African American—out-homered Babe Ruth, most fans praised him through 21 All-Star seasons—more appearances than any other player.

Aaron held the record for most career home runs for 32 years, until Barry Bonds reached 756 in 2006.

The best batters have strength, speed, a good eye, and quick reflexes. With only a half second to swing, batters must also be confident and ready.

Balls and Strikes

Batters try to hit a pitch into the field of play—the area between the white lines that extend away from home plate. Batters must swing at any pitch inside the strike zone or be charged with a strike. Hitting the ball **foul** and swinging and missing are also strikes. Three strikes put the batter out. Pitches outside the strike zone are called balls. If a pitcher throws four balls before three strikes, the batter gets a **walk** to first base.

strike zone

The strike zone is the imaginary rectangular area over home plate that reaches from the batter's knees to armpits.

Hits and RBIs

A batted ball is only called a hit when the batter is able to reach first base before being put out. Runners already on a base will also try to advance to the next base or even further. Any teammate who reaches home plate on a batter's hit gives that batter a "run batted in," or RBI.

The New York Yankees' Alex Rodriguez—shown here batting against the Kansas City Royals—had more than 1,800 career RBIs by 2010, one of the highest numbers among active players in Major League Baseball.

17

The Batting Order

Each team bats in a set order chosen by the manager before the game. Nine players bat in sequence and then start again at the beginning. A team bats until it gets three outs. Batters continue where they left off in the order next inning.

Top of the Order

The first three batters come up each time through the order, so they're likely to get one more at-bat than later batters. They need to be dependable hitters with high batting averages. Their consistent hitting loads up the bases with runners. They're usually followed by hitters with more power who can bring in a lot of runs.

In 2010, the St. Louis Cardinals moved Matt Holliday from fourth to second in the batting lineup. Holliday responded by hitting more home runs and RBIs.

18

Many fans consider Ichiro Suzuki of the Seattle Mariners to be one of the best leadoff batters in Major League Baseball.

The very first batter in the lineup is called the leadoff batter. This player is usually one of the best hitters on the team. His job is to try to hit a **single** or otherwise get on base. Leadoff batters are often fast runners who can round the bases or even **steal** them to score an early run.

The fourth, fifth, and sixth batters are where the power hitters are. Their job is to score runs by hitting the ball well enough and far enough that the base runners ahead of them can reach home plate. The middle hitters are sometimes slower, but they make up for it by hitting the ball deep, possibly for home runs.

Power hitter Mark Reynolds of the Arizona Diamondbacks usually bats fifth or sixth. Here he is shown hitting a two-run homer against the San Diego Padres.

The fourth batter is sometimes called the "cleanup" batter. This is because he's the most likely batter to hit a home run and "clean runners off" the bases by advancing them around to home plate. The cleanup batter is the team's strongest hitter. As a threat to hit deep, he's often the team's best scoring opportunity.

The Detroit Tigers' cleanup man Miguel Cabrera hits a home run in the ninth inning against the New York Yankees.

The Chicago White Sox's Alexei Ramirez is one of the best bottom-of-the-order batters in the major leagues.

Bottom of the Order

Even the best fielders still need to be good batters. Strong defensive players with lower batting averages commonly end up at the bottom of the order. They're often easier to get out, and they usually get fewer walks because pitchers try to strike them out. Even so, these batters must try for hits in order to set up the top of the order, who are waiting "on deck."

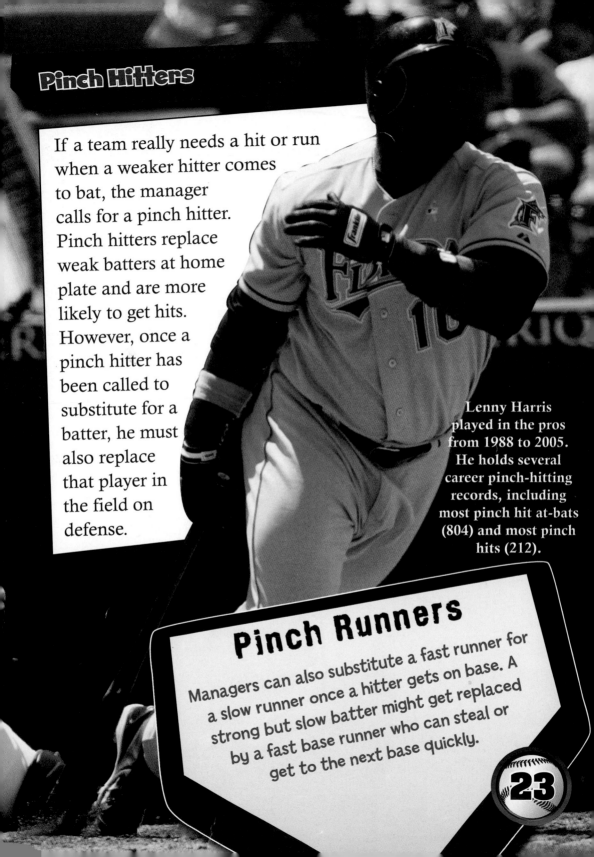

If a team really needs a hit or run when a weaker hitter comes to bat, the manager calls for a pinch hitter. Pinch hitters replace weak batters at home plate and are more likely to get hits. However, once a pinch hitter has been called to substitute for a batter, he must also replace that player in the field on defense.

Lenny Harris played in the pros from 1988 to 2005. He holds several career pinch-hitting records, including most pinch hit at-bats (804) and most pinch hits (212).

Pinch Runners

Managers can also substitute a fast runner for a slow runner once a hitter gets on base. A strong but slow batter might get replaced by a fast base runner who can steal or get to the next base quickly.

KEY SKILLS

More than any other skill on the baseball field, batting can be learned. Here are some of the basics.

Taking a Stand

Batters stand on either side of home plate in an area called the "batter's box." Batters with long arms might stand back to better cover the plate. Standing back in the box gives batters a tiny bit longer to react to the pitch. Standing forward in the box makes it more likely that hits will be fair balls. Each batter develops a personal stance, or position, that gets him the most hits.

Chipper Jones of the Atlanta Braves is one of the best switch hitters of all time.

24

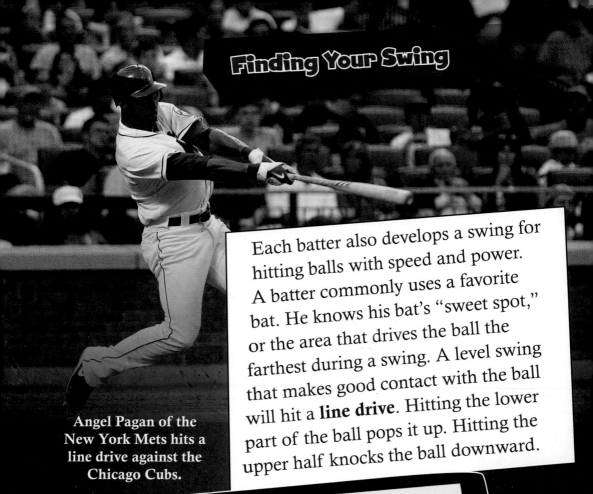

Each batter also develops a swing for hitting balls with speed and power. A batter commonly uses a favorite bat. He knows his bat's "sweet spot," or the area that drives the ball the farthest during a swing. A level swing that makes good contact with the ball will hit a **line drive**. Hitting the lower part of the ball pops it up. Hitting the upper half knocks the ball downward.

Angel Pagan of the New York Mets hits a line drive against the Chicago Cubs.

Switch Hitting

Pitchers have an advantage when pitching against opposite-handed batters. It's easier for them to throw the ball in close to the batter, where it's harder to hit. However, some batters learn to hit from either side of the plate to remove that advantage. This is called "switch hitting."

Batters don't need to be really fast runners, but it certainly helps. A half second can be the difference between a hit and an out at first base. Fast runners can round the bases more quickly and perhaps turn a single into a double. Not only does getting extra bases mean the batter is closer to home, but also that he's protected against a **force out** when the next batter hits.

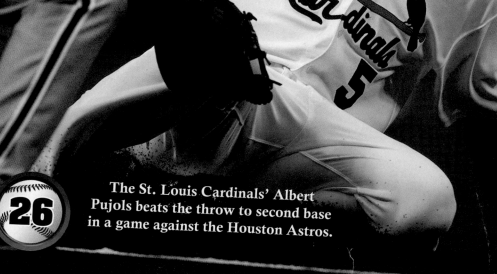

The St. Louis Cardinals' Albert Pujols beats the throw to second base in a game against the Houston Astros.

Hits only help the team when they turn into runs. Even if a batter gets an RBI or two on a hit, he wants to get to home plate, too. He watches his coaches for the signs to steal or run. An alert runner with good timing can get a jump on the pitch or hit and advance safely.

The Colorado Rockies' Carlos Gonzalez sprints to third as he watches a hit sail into the outfield.

POWER PLAYS

Hitting the ball high and deep looks great, but it doesn't help if an outfielder catches the ball for an out. Power hitters have a few things to keep in mind.

Home-Run Hitting

Batters usually hit home runs by swinging with all their might at a good pitch. Even then, batters need control. Home-run hitters often pull their hits to one side of the outfield. The walls there are closer to home plate, so the ball has a better chance of going over. Balls must travel much further to clear the center-field wall.

Evan Longoria hits a home run for the Tampa Bay Rays.

A home run lets the batter and any runners currently on base come in to score. If the bases are "loaded," which means there's a runner on every base, that's a total of four runs. This highest-scoring hit is called a "grand slam."

Lou Gehrig hitting a home run

Lou Gehrig

Home runs and grand slams helped New York Yankee Lou Gehrig bring in hundreds of RBIs. Gehrig holds the record for most career grand slams with 23.

THE SOFT TOUCH

Batting isn't all about power. It's also about controlling where a ball is hit and how fast it flies.

Contact Hitting

A contact hitter is a batter who's good at "protecting the plate." This means that they hold off for a split second to see if a pitch will be a strike, and then use a quick "chop swing" to hit balls in the strike zone. By using quick, controlled swings, the batter punches the ball through holes in the infield or arcs a hit to the space between the infielders and outfielders. Contact hitters aren't usually known for power hitting, but they're less likely to strike out.

Michael Cuddyer is a versatile contact hitter with the Minnesota Twins.

The bunt is a useful tool for advancing runners. In a bunting situation, the batter holds his bat out in front of him across the plate like a barrier. He backs the wide part of the bat with one hand to direct the pitch down toward the ground. If it bounces properly—high and close to the plate—the defense may not have time to throw the runner out. The batter may or may not make it to first, but the bunt is often used as a **sacrifice** play to allow other runners to advance or score.

Derek Jeter of the New York Yankees bunts during a game against the Baltimore Orioles.

31

BATTING PRACTICE

Batters need to work on their swing until it becomes second nature. It's hard to think about the game and a swing at the same time. Practicing helps.

Bulking Up

Batters lift weights to help their power and quickness. With proper exercise, their stronger arms can swing the bat faster. Bat speed is more important than strength for good hitting. Many batters take practice swings with a ringed weight on their bat so it feels lighter and swings faster when they swing at pitches.

Joe Mauer of the Minnesota Twins practices his swing "on deck" while a teammate is at bat against the Chicago White Sox.

32

The Milwaukee Brewers' Prince Fielder watches his home run hit sail over the fence in a game against the Pittsburgh Pirates.

Mind the Mound

Batters study the habits of pitchers to know how fast they can throw, what pitches they use, and what their throws look like. Being able to guess the next pitch can give batters a better chance to hit it. Batters often practice with their own pitchers or with pitching machines to prepare for certain pitches.

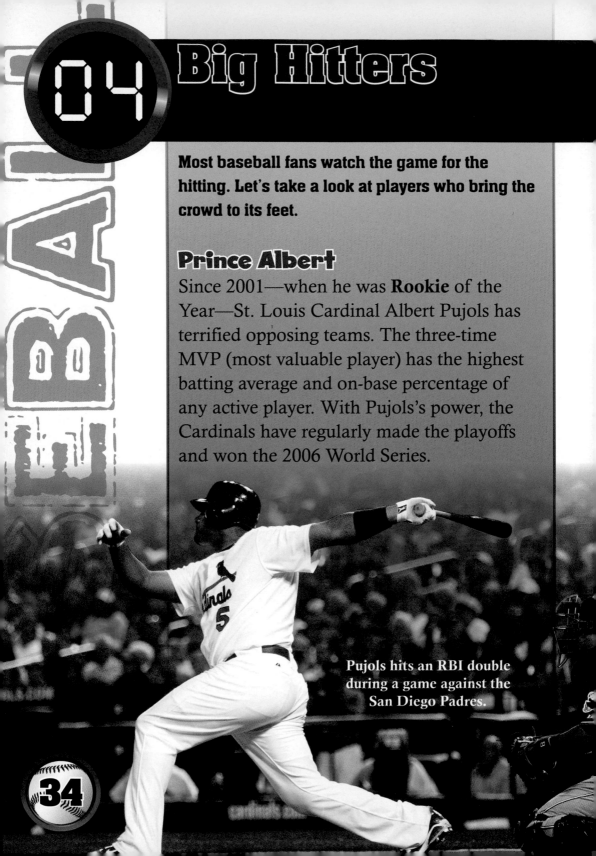

04

Big Hitters

Most baseball fans watch the game for the hitting. Let's take a look at players who bring the crowd to its feet.

Prince Albert

Since 2001—when he was **Rookie** of the Year—St. Louis Cardinal Albert Pujols has terrified opposing teams. The three-time MVP (most valuable player) has the highest batting average and on-base percentage of any active player. With Pujols's power, the Cardinals have regularly made the playoffs and won the 2006 World Series.

Pujols hits an RBI double during a game against the San Diego Padres.

Playing for the Minnesota Twins, Justin Morneau isn't too far away from his native Canada. From 2006 to 2009, Morneau batted in 100 or more runs per season. The 2006 American League MVP has also won two Silver Sluggers—an award given to the best batter at each position every year.

Morneau prepares for a pitch in a game against the Oakland Athletics.

A-Rod was the youngest player to reach 500 and 600 home runs.

A-Rod

Alexander Rodriguez is one of only seven players who have hit more than 600 home runs. His "A Bombs" have led the league in home runs five times. "A-Rod," as his fans call him, has averaged more than 40 home runs a season since 1996. He's also a three-time MVP and a 10-time Silver Slugger winner.

One of the top cleanup hitters in the game is Miguel Cabrera. He has earned more than 100 RBIs every full season he's played and has had a batting average near or over .300 nearly every year. With his combination of sharp hitting and solid power, Cabrera could be the first player to earn a "triple crown" in more than 40 years.

Cabrera is a two-time Silver Slugger winner. He also won a World Series Championship with the Florida Marlins in 2003.

Game Changer

The Texas Rangers' Josh Hamilton is the sort of player who can take over a game. Hamilton leads the offense by driving in runs and getting on base multiple times a game. He has been one of the top producers in the league in hits and RBIs since 2008, when he drove in a league-leading 130 runs and won a Silver Slugger Award.

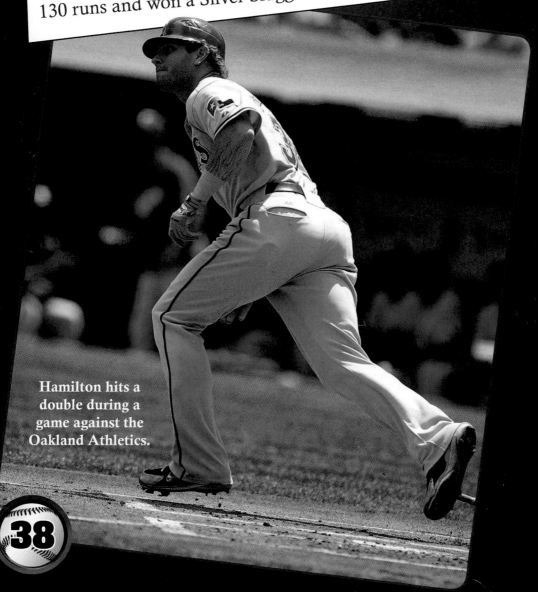

Hamilton hits a double during a game against the Oakland Athletics.

Here is Howard getting a hit during the 81st MLB All-Star Game in 2010.

Young Gun

Ryan Howard has reached the 100-run and 200-run marks faster than any other player. The Philadelphia Phillies' batter has a left-handed pull so strong that opposing defenses sometimes move all their players over toward right field. Howard began his career as the 2005 Rookie of the Year and went on to win an MVP, two home-run titles, three RBI titles, and a World Series Championship.

39

05

Future Star: You!

Hope to hit it big some day? Then use the following tips and swing for the fences!

Tee Time

Pros still use batting tees to work on their swing, and you should, too. Set the ball to different heights in your strike zone. Practice until you can hit line drives cleanly off your bat's sweet spot. Experiment with opening your stance by moving your front foot closer to or farther from the tee to work on directing your hits left or right. Pay attention to your stance and swing as you hit the ball so you can apply them to real pitches.

Pitch Position

If you're setting up on a ball field, put the tee in front of home plate. Remember that you're trying to hit pitches as they reach the plate, not as they pass over it.

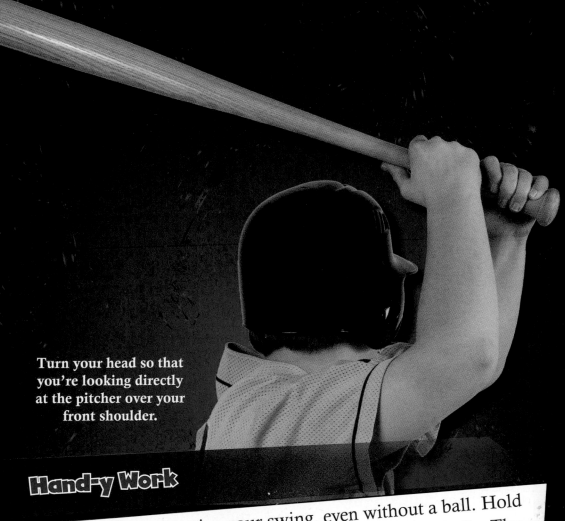

Turn your head so that you're looking directly at the pitcher over your front shoulder.

Hand-y Work

You can always practice your swing, even without a ball. Hold your bat with your lower hand at the knob on the handle. The fingers on both hands should touch and line up along the handle. Use your fingers more than your palms to hold the bat to free up your wrists for more power. Raise your elbows up and out slightly to let your arms make full swings. If you want more control with a little less power, "choke up" by moving your hands slightly higher up the handle.

When bunting, aim the ball toward first or third and not toward the pitcher.

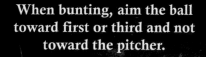

Lay Down the Bunt

You can practice your bunt stance at any time, too. Stand at the plate as you would before any pitch. Step in with your back foot and turn on your right foot until your shoulders face the pitcher square, then hunch slightly. At the same time, slide your inside hand up to the middle of the bat's "barrel." Keep your fingers under or behind the bat for safety. Angle the bat up slightly at the top of your strike zone to hit balls downward. Practice making this move as quickly as possible.

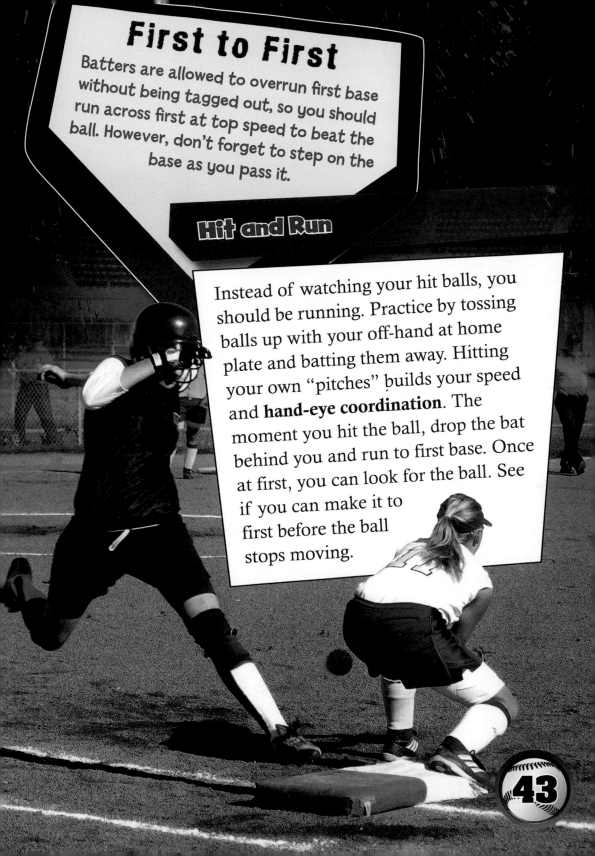

First to First

Batters are allowed to overrun first base without being tagged out, so you should run across first at top speed to beat the ball. However, don't forget to step on the base as you pass it.

Hit and Run

Instead of watching your hit balls, you should be running. Practice by tossing balls up with your off-hand at home plate and batting them away. Hitting your own "pitches" builds your speed and **hand-eye coordination**. The moment you hit the ball, drop the bat behind you and run to first base. Once at first, you can look for the ball. See if you can make it to first before the ball stops moving.

Record Book

Do you want to know who the best batters in the history of baseball are? The following lists show how the best of the best measure up.

Hank Aaron

Highest Career Batting Average:

1. Ty Cobb	.366	left-handed
2. Rogers Hornsby	.359	right-handed
3. "Shoeless" Joe Jackson	.356	left-handed
4. "Lefty" O'Doul	.349	left-handed
5. Ed Delahanty	.347	right-handed

Most Career RBIs:

1. Hank Aaron	2,297	right-handed
2. Babe Ruth	2,213	left-handed
3. "Cap" Anson	2,075	right-handed
4. Barry Bonds	1,996	left-handed
5. Lou Gehrig	1,995	left-handed

Most Single-Season RBIs:

1. "Hack" Wilson	191	1930	right-handed
2. Lou Gehrig	184	1931	left-handed
3. Hank Greenberg	183	1937	right-handed
4. Lou Gehrig	175	1927	left-handed
Jimmie Foxx	175	1938	right-handed

Most Career Home Runs:

1. Barry Bonds	762	left-handed
2. Hank Aaron	755	right-handed
3. Babe Ruth	714	left-handed
4. Willie Mays	660	right-handed
5. Ken Griffey Jr.	630	left-handed

Ichiro Suzuki

Most Career Hits:

1. Pete Rose	4,256	switch hitter
2. Ty Cobb	4,189	left-handed
3. Hank Aaron	3,771	right-handed
4. Stan Musial	3,630	left-handed
5. Tris Speaker	3,514	left-handed

Most Single-Season Hits:

1. Ichiro Suzuki (*still active*)	262	2004	left-handed
2. George Sisler	257	1920	left-handed
3. "Lefty" O'Doul	254	1929	left-handed
Bill Terry	254	1930	left-handed
5. Al Simmons	253	1925	right-handed

45

Glossary

batting average: the number of hits a batter has divided by his opportunities at bat

defense: the team trying to stop the other team from scoring

double: a hit during which a batter makes it to and stays on second base without being put out

force out: putting out a runner by getting the ball to the player guarding the base the runner must go to because of other runners coming behind him

foul: a ball that is hit outside the lines extending from home plate, which define the field of play

hand-eye coordination: the ability to use vision to guide your hand to grab or touch an object

inning: a unit of play in which both teams have a chance to bat until recording three outs

interleague: something done between two teams from different leagues

line drive: a level hit ball that does not travel up or down very much as it flies

Negro League: one of several baseball leagues for African American players that existed from the late 1800s to the mid-1900s, when African Americans were allowed to play in the major leagues

offense: the team trying to score

on-base percentage: the number of times a batter gets on base through normal play—including walks—divided by his opportunities at bat

RBI: run batted in, or a run that is driven in by a batter

rookie: a player in his first year in a league

sacrifice: a giving up of something, which allows someone else to receive something

single: a hit during which a batter makes it to and stays on first base without being put out

slugging percentage: the number of bases a batter gets from his hits divided by his opportunities at bat

steal: to advance to the next base successfully without the batter first hitting the ball

triple: a hit during which a batter makes it to and stays on third base without being put out

walk: free passage to first base as a result of being pitched four balls before three strikes

For More Information

Books

Bowen, Fred. *Winners Take All*. Atlanta, GA: Peachtree Publishers, 2009.

Buckley, James. *Baseball*. New York, NY: DK Publishing, 2010.

Christopher, Matt. *The Hit-Away Kid*. Chicago, IL: Norwood House Press, 2010.

Dreier, David. *Baseball: How It Works*. Mankato, MN: Capstone Press, 2010.

Jacobs, Greg. *The Everything Kids' Baseball Book*. Avon, MA: Adams Media, 2010.

Lupica, Mike. *The Batboy*. New York, NY: Philomel Books, 2010.

Web Sites

Club MLB
web.clubmlb.com
Major League Baseball's activity-filled site has games and interactive fun features to teach kids about baseball and its past and present players.

Kids' Club
mlb.mlb.com/mlb/kids/index.jsp
Major League Baseball's information site for kids who want to learn more about how to be a better player or want to write to their favorite player. The site also provides links to the pages of each Major League Baseball team.

National Baseball Hall of Fame
baseballhall.org
The Web site for the National Baseball Hall of Fame in Cooperstown, New York, tells the in-depth history of the game. Learn about the achievements of some of the finest players and personalities from more than 200 hundred years of baseball.

Index

About the Author

Jason Glaser is a freelance writer and stay-at-home father living in Mankato, Minnesota. He has written over fifty nonfiction books for children, including books on sports stars such as Jackie Robinson. As a youngster playing youth baseball, he once completed an unassisted triple play, which is the highlight of his sports career.